Feral Cat Rescue

Tips and Techniques
for Caregivers

Casey Wright

For "Soldier"

The victim of two separate car accidents, Soldier was found with a shattered foot and a tail broken in several places. He was one year old and feral, and the treating veterinarian advised that Soldier should be kept indoors because he would need ongoing treatment for his conditions.

It took fifteen months to socialize him, but Soldier is now one of the friendliest cats in Casey Wright's foster home. He needs medicine twice a day for constipation, which is a result of his broken tail and consequent nerve damage. He *loves* the medicine because it gets stirred into that magic substance, chicken baby food.

CONTENTS

ACKNOWLEDGMENTS

The fantastic photo on the cover, the one shown below, and the picture on page 14 were all taken by a kind and generous photographer named Carolyn Allmacher. Used with permission.

DISCLAIMER

Injuries caused by feral cats can be extremely dangerous, even deadly, for humans. The suggestions in this book are based on the opinions and observations of one individual with many years of experience dealing with feral cats. Advice given here is not intended for complete novices, nor is it intended to replace common sense and good judgment. Readers are urged to exercise utmost caution.

Medical treatments described in this book should be used under the guidance and supervision of a veterinarian.

INTRODUCTION

Feral cats are a special sort. Working with them requires an enormous amount of emotional strength, given that for their entire lifetimes they want nothing to do with the humans who so lovingly care for them on a daily basis. By definition, feral cats are wild; they keep their distance even when they're starving and food would be the reward for closer contact.

Some readers will say, "Yes, but I can pet some of the cats in my feral colony." If that is the case, then those cats are not truly feral – instead, we refer to them as "strays." They most likely had some contact with humans when they were kittens, but they are undersocialized and a trap would be needed in order to catch them.

There is also the type of cat that wanders into a feral colony or back-yard and begs for food, perhaps even trying to enter a home, or rubbing furiously against the legs of any human who might offer food. It's easy to pop them into a carrier for a trip to the vet. These cats aren't feral, either. We refer to them as "friendly strays."

While there are a few tips in this book that concern the handling of all cats, including strays of varying levels of socialization, what will be addressed here is primarily the safe and humane care of feral kittens and cats while trapping, as well as during captivity for medical treatment, recovery, and fostering.

Other care issues, such as feeding and maintaining feral cat colonies and understanding the premises and basics of "trap neuter return" (TNR) practices, are beyond the scope of this book. Much information can be obtained from Alley Cat Allies; several shelters around the country post helpful information on their websites. *The Stray Cat Handbook* (Howell, 1999) by Tamara Kreuz is another good resource, although some of the content is outdated.

CHAPTER 1

CATCHING FERAL CATS

This book assumes that you already know something about feral cats, and that you want to learn some advanced handling techniques and new methods of caring for them in the most humane and safe way possible.

Veterinarians and their technicians might be tempted to skip this chapter, but reading it can give them an idea of what rescuers go through *just to get a cat to the clinic.* The rule of thumb that I've calculated is that it takes an average of ten hours of time to prepare, trap, transport, recover, and release each feral cat that gets spayed or neutered. It's hard work.

Choosing and Using Appropriate Equipment

Regular traps, also referred to as humane traps, work best on new colonies where trapping has never been done before. On the first day of trapping at one such backyard colony where an elderly woman had been feeding cats for years, we placed several traps at various locations around the property and just stood by the front door listening to the doors closing *snap snap snap.*

My trapping partner and I refer to our favorite style of regular traps as "guillotine traps," because the panel of one end can be raised, lowered, or removed as needed. Tomahawk sells a nice one – Model 606. Its relatively small size makes it easy to carry and to fit into the car, and despite the size it will accommodate even the largest tomcat. In the next two chapters, you will see why this type of trap is so convenient for both trappers and veterinary staff alike.

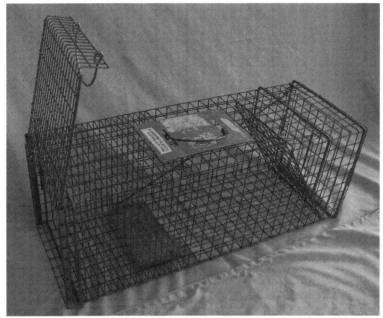

A humane "guillotine trap" with the door raised.

There are sundry ways to prepare a trap; most cat rescuers have their favorite methods. But after trying several different techniques, we prefer the following:

🐾 Line the bottom of the trap with a sturdy piece of cardboard, being careful not to let it touch the trip plate or obstruct the door from closing properly. Some trappers cover almost the entire floor of the trap (including the trip plate) with newspaper, but in our experience it rattles too much when the weather is windy and spooks the cats. And personally, I find the reason that trappers want to cover the trip plate amusing – they don't want the cat to see it. As though a cat would really know what it was! We've also seen trappers use fabric but again, windy weather is problematic.

🐾 Cover the trap with a large bath towel or sheet. Both the body of the trap and the closed end should be covered if you're trying to catch kittens, but adults are more likely to go into the trap if the end opposite the opening isn't covered. The theory is that the cats think they can easily escape if they can see out the opposite end of the trap as they enter.

🐾 Make sure the trap is working properly, and that the closed end of the trap is securely locked. We've all lost cats by forgetting these crucial steps. There is one exception, however: when trapping after dark, *do not* lock the closed end. That way, if a raccoon or skunk gets trapped, the guillotine door can easily be lifted with a long stick or broom handle. Just remember to lock the closed end before transporting a freshly caught cat.

🐾 Use enticing wet food as bait. Some trappers talk about sardines and such, but we've had the best luck with smelly cat food (such as Fancy Feast "tuna and shrimp") or plain old human-grade tuna in oil (the oil prevents the tuna from drying out). Place the bait on a plastic lid, like the ones that cover tubs of margarine – a plastic lid won't hurt the cat if it thrashes around after capture. Make sure that the plastic lid will not slide under the trip plate and prevent it from functioning properly.

🐾 *WARNING:* Never open a can of cat food and simply place it as-is in the trap. Cats can severely injure themselves by slicing their tongues or cheeks on the sharp lip of the can.

🐾 Check your traps every 30-45 minutes, and never leave traps unattended for long periods of time; especially not overnight.

When a target cat absolutely refuses to go into a regular trap no matter how long you've starved it, then it's time to bring out a drop trap. Drop traps measure about three feet square and one foot high. The bottom is open. The trapper props up one edge of the trap with a stick that has a long string secured to the bottom. Food is placed at the back of the trap; in other words, near the side of the trap that rests on the ground. It is crucial to center the food between the sides of the trap so that the trap doesn't fall on a cat's body.

As soon as the cat that you want to catch goes under the drop trap and starts eating, you pull the string and the trap falls over the cat. (Video demonstrations can be found on YouTube.) Immediately covering the drop trap with a thick blanket that reaches the ground on all sides will keep the cat calm until you can line up a regular trap. Using a trap door that is installed on one side of the drop trap, you then transfer the cat into a regular trap.

When the transfer process is being done by one person working alone, it can be difficult coaxing the cat into the regular trap while simultaneously holding both traps firmly in position. Short bungee cords can be used to temporarily secure the guillotine trap to the drop trap and prevent the cat from escaping.

*Photo of a drop trap in action. Always wait for the target cat
to start eating before pulling the string.*

This process sounds relatively easy, but it is not. The whole thing is incredibly time consuming, because the trapper must be present during every single second of trapping. Uneven ground can offer a panicked cat room to squeeze under the side of the drop trap and evade capture. A fair amount of agility and strength on the part of the trapper is necessary in order to get the trap set up and to handle the transfer process from the drop trap to the regular trap. And it's unfortunately rather easy for a feral cat to escape during the transfer process.

It is particularly risky to use a drop trap when trying to catch feral kittens under the age of eight weeks. They dart around so quickly that they can get caught under the edge of the trap and be crushed. Drop trapping young kittens should be done only as a last resort.

The good aspects of using drop traps include the fact that you *can* usually catch a cat that is "trap savvy" (i.e., avoids regular humane traps), and you can trap multiple cats simultaneously. Employing a drop trap works well on an established colony because the process allows other cats that have already been spayed or neutered to eat during trapping sessions. But be careful what you wish for: in one case, we used a drop trap at a previously stable 15-cat colony where two new cats had shown up; one was injured. During three days of trapping, we went through 42 cans of cat food! Accustomed to getting mostly dry food, the existing fifteen cats really enjoyed themselves.

How do you obtain a drop trap? Tomahawk and Tru-Trap now sell drop traps, but I've never used them myself. (The Tomahawk trap has the aforementioned bungee cords already attached.) Several homemade designs are available on the Internet; HubCats provides a great build-your-own tutorial.

The drop trap shown in our photo was custom-made by a woman who thought our original one was too flimsy. She used kitchen shelving for the sides and top, bungee cords to hold it together, and installed a modified pet door in the side panel.

Preparation

In order to catch a cat, it must be motivated to eat in an alien environment – either in a humane trap, or under your drop trap. The warier the cat, the hungrier it must be. While in some trapping locations you can feed cats in unset traps to acclimate them to eating in an unfamiliar place, at most trapping sites this is impossible to do (for example, when trapping in a commercial parking lot, your traps might get stolen when unattended). Thus, while you are trapping, withholding of food and daily drop trapping for up to five straight days might be necessary in order to catch a wary feral cat.

Whether you undertake the acclimation process or want to start trapping "cold," it will be necessary to get food sources under control. During the days leading up to your trapping event, prepare by talking not only with regular feeders, but also with people who live and work around your trapping site. Tell them what you are doing, why you are doing it, and ask them if they know of anyone who feeds stray cats.

You might be tempted to skip this step, but you risk wasting an enormous amount of time and energy if you do. If there is just one old granny around the corner who puts food out once a day, you'll be sabotaged; your target kitties will never go into your traps. Think of it this way – cats *can* get food for themselves, whether by catching mice or an occasional bird, or by rummaging through garbage cans. You're only going to catch your target cat if she hasn't managed to find food anywhere else; you don't need Granny adding to your problem.

There was one feral cat colony where even our best preparation efforts were foiled. My trapping partner and I were trying to catch a three-year untrappable female named Blue. (We have no idea how old she was; all we knew was that people had spent three years trying to trap her.) Despite all we had done to alert neighbors and feeders about our planned trapping activities, each time we arrived at the site there was food *everywhere*. It turned out that we had a compulsive feeder trying to sabotage our efforts (she didn't want us to "starve" the cats). So we enlisted several friends and made sure that every two hours someone would remove any food that the feeder had squirreled away under the bushes. In order to keep the feeder off balance, we trapped at completely random times. One of my friends is an extremely early riser, so he accompanied me to the site at 5 a.m.; my trapping partner went the next night after dark. It took five straight days of trapping, but we got Blue.

Timing

Schedule adequate time for the job. I usually start on a Sunday, because spay/neuter services where I live are available only Monday through Friday. Block out the entire week; in other words, you have to be able to go to the trapping site at least once a day, for a minimum of two hours each time, for five straight days. And it is best if you *don't* go at the same time every day, because you never know what kind of stimuli might prevent a cat from venturing into a trap – or encourage it to go in.

There's an interesting story about this: a local cat rescue team had worked for an entire summer doing TNR in an industrial area just south of where I live. They had trapped almost 50 cats, but one intact (unspayed) female was proving herself completely resistant to all of their tricks. The rescue group asked me to help, but it was mid-week, and I had a work obligation in the middle of the following week. The only option was to start trapping on a Wednesday and hope I could catch her quickly.

Of course, I didn't. Despite my use of a drop trap, she was as elusive as the other trappers had reported. So we fed the cats on Friday and I asked the feeder to withhold food on Saturday night, returning to the site on Sunday. Now I was starting all over again.

Unbeknownst to me, a mechanic rented one of the car bays in the building and worked on friends' cars in his spare time. Late Sunday afternoon he showed up; my heart sank, because I had counted on the area being quiet. About a half hour after he arrived, things got worse: a large truck pulled in towing a car behind it. Two guys got out and strolled over to talk with the mechanic, leaving the tow truck running. I was silently fuming at their noisy intrusion.

Certain that the commotion would scare Mama Cat off, I went to check on the regular traps that I had set in various locations around the industrial complex. After I had finished and rounded the corner towards my car, I couldn't believe my eyes. With all that chaos, there was Mama Cat eating under the drop trap! Thank goodness the passenger-side window of my car was open. I leaned into the car head first, grabbed the string, and pulled as hard as I could. Got her!

And then I couldn't get her transferred into the regular trap. She had beaten herself up when the trap dropped, and was panicked and bleeding from the nose. One of the truck drivers came over and, without a word, gently and kindly helped steer Mama Cat into the regular trap; then turned on his heels and walked back to his truck. He didn't say a word about the cat's bloody nose. Wonder what he was thinking.

Placing Traps

It's crucial to think like a cat both when you're putting out regular traps, or trying to find the best spot for a drop trap. The essential component of both is that cats want to feel that they are protected overhead.

When placing traps, I look for any kind of covering available. Perhaps it's the leaves of a large hydrangea bush; maybe the branches of a tree, the eaves of a house, or the roof of a carport; in one case, it was the shelf of a barbeque grill. In other words, the overhead protection doesn't need to be close by – the tree branches were 12 feet up! And it doesn't need to be large – the shelf of the barbeque grill was only about one foot square.

As usual, there are exceptions. In one case, I was asked to help with a 10-year untrappable cat named Mama Mia. She was a gorgeous medium-haired Siamese mix who lived in a commercial parking lot and kept having litter after litter of kittens. She was immune to any kind of regular trap, and had avoided a drop trap as well. (One trapper tried until 3 a.m. to get Mama Mia, only to return home empty-handed.)

I used all of my tricks with overhead protection, and nothing was working. On the fifth day of trapping, I decided to switch to *side* protection. There were two concrete bump-outs from the building. One housed the garbage dumpster and recycling containers, and the other housed the noisy heating and air conditioning equipment. I placed the drop trap in the 6-foot space between the bump-outs, and Mama Mia was under the trap in less than five minutes.

Miscellaneous trapping tips:

When kittens are involved and the mother needs to be trapped, *always* catch the mother first and *then* the kittens. Time and again I hear about trappers or kindly neighbors who capture kittens (especially those under three weeks old that are relatively easy to handle) and only then try to catch the mother. Sensing danger, once her babies have been removed from the nest, most mother cats will leave the area and will not return for several weeks – if at all – by which time she is likely to be pregnant again. If, however, the mother is a stray that is not completely afraid of humans, it is sometimes possible to put the kittens into a carrier and place the carrier door facing the food end of a trap, covering both the carrier and the trap with a large beach towel. In many cases, the mother will enter the trap in an attempt to get to her babies.

As for your trapping attire, be sure to wear adequate clothing. Pants made of thick fabric such as jean material, as well as a good pair of socks, will protect your ankles and legs from brambles and poisonous weeds.

Keep a coat or thick sweatshirt handy in case the weather changes while you're trapping. Sneakers or leather shoes are a must – one tomcat reached out from under the drop trap and attacked my foot. His toenail put a large gouge in the thick leather upper of the shoe, but my foot was safe.

Another absolute necessity is a powerful flashlight. It will help you see into traps when night has fallen before you've finished trapping. In one location where a group of us was trapping, we didn't realize that the lights from the street didn't reach a secluded spot where we had hidden a trap. We couldn't see a blasted thing. I had to go all the way home, get a flashlight, and return to the site to retrieve the trap.

Last but not least, much literature on trapping advises to clean humane traps and disinfect them with bleach between use. If you live in an area where ringworm or distemper are rampant, this might be advisable. But under normal trapping conditions, these actions will make a trap smell like humans. Only in cases of true filth (such as contact with feces) do I wash off my traps, and then I use only a mild detergent and rinse extremely well. Otherwise, it's best simply to let your traps smell like cats!

CHAPTER 2

HANDLING FERAL CATS

Working with ferals can be a fairly dangerous and unpredictable venture, both for you and for the cats. So many things can happen! While certain issues will be addressed in this section, there are a few over-arching rules to keep in mind:

🐾 *Always* keep feral cats fully covered. Once you've trapped a cat, check the sides and ends of the trap to make sure that the towel reaches the ground so that no daylight is showing. Darkness will keep cats calm and feeling protected, lessening the chances that they will injure themselves by trying to escape, and minimizing the possibility that they will lash out at some unsuspecting human.

🐾 *Always* move fluidly when working with feral cats. One of my volunteers calls this my "zen-like state." Jerky movements or anything that creates the slightest noise can scare and provoke an already-terrified cat. Even lifting the towel to look at the cat should be done slowly, giving the cat time to move away from you inside the trap.

🐾 Remember the lesson that was drilled into my head as a child living on a farm: *the animals are more afraid of you than you are of them.* Feeling nervous and being cautious keep you alert and protected, but you can't allow the animals to sense fear on your part. This balancing act of feeling one way and behaving another can be difficult to achieve, but it is a crucial skill in working with feral cats.

With the fundamentals in place, it's good to have other techniques in your pocket that you can use when the time is right. Please note that these techniques are not for the faint of heart, and should not be used if you do not feel comfortable with them. Try them out on a moderately skittish cat before attempting them when you have a true feral on your hands.

Pre-surgery Evaluation and Care

Once you have a cat in a trap, you need to get it ready for surgery. If you are lucky enough to have spay/neuter services available the following day, then for the safety of all concerned, the cat should stay in the trap. Unfortunately, this limits the extent to which you can assess the health and temperament of the cat — but there are a few things that you can do.

First, listen for any sounds from the cat. Meowing means that the cat probably is a stray (previously handled by humans) rather than a true feral. Feral mother cats teach their kittens to be completely quiet so as not to attract predators. As an interesting side note, many visitors to my foster home ask me why it's so quiet, perhaps expecting a bunch of meowing felines to greet them at the door. It's because for the most part, all of my furry friends were born feral!

Next, place the trap, with the towel over it, in an area that has good lighting. A flashlight can sometimes help you see even better. Gently lift one side of the towel. Examine the cat for an "ear tip" or notch. (Removal of one-quarter inch of the tip of a cat's ear, or making a V-shaped notch on the ear, is the sign of an altered feral cat.) If there isn't adequate contrast — perhaps both the cat's fur and the towel are dark in color — you might need to use a different towel. An ear tip on an adult cat can be extremely difficult to spot unless you're at the proper angle and can look at the ears against a contrasting background.

In this regard, my fellow cat rescuers enjoy ribbing me about one particular situation. I was at the local humane society clinic on a Friday morning and overheard an elderly couple talking to the receptionist. The receptionist was patiently explaining that they didn't have room to accept any more feral cats for surgery that day. The elderly couple reiterated that they didn't know what to do with the cat, as it was a holiday weekend. They felt it would be cruel to hold the cat in a trap for four days.

I stepped forward and told them that I would take care of the cat, running it into a roomy cage for its weekend stay, and would bring it back to the clinic on Tuesday. Funny, but I took their word for it that the cat needed to be neutered and never bothered checking myself. On Monday it finally occurred to me to examine the ears and *voilà*, the cat was missing the tip of his left ear. Poor fellow was very happy to be returned to his outdoor home that afternoon.

Feral cat with a left "ear tip."

While you're looking to see if a cat has an ear tip or notch, take a look at its eyes and nose. If there is any yellow or green discharge, then you should either a) mentally prepare yourself that you will have to hold the cat after surgery to medicate it, or b) take the cat to a clinic that has Convenia on hand. (Convenia is an injectable, 14-day antibiotic.) The latter option is obviously the less stressful of the two. Incidentally, if you note any reddish-brown discharge, this is typically *not* something that will need any medical treatment. Oxidization makes normal cat tears turn this color.

As a side note, there are a couple of other important considerations when choosing the clinic to which you take feral cats for spay/neuter surgery. You should know whether the clinic staff uses an anesthesia "cocktail," or whether they simply administer isoflurane. The difference can be dramatic.

With the anesthesia "cocktail" method, veterinary technicians give cats an injectable anesthesia to make the cats docile while being prepared for surgery. Only during the surgery itself do they then knock the cat out with inhaled isoflurane. *Any cat with a heart condition can die from this routine.* Because it is impossible to check a feral cat's heartbeat until the cat is under some type of sedation, over the years we have lost a few cats to this treatment. In addition, rescuers should remember that it takes a few hours for the inject-able anesthesia to wear off, so it is important to keep the cats in a quiet place during that time. Cats should be fed only a small amount of food at first, because a certain amount of nausea can accompany the wakening process.

In contrast to the anesthesia "cocktail" method, some clinics run cats into a plexiglas anesthesia induction chamber and administer isoflurane only. One veterinarian I know refers to this as "boxing" the cats. This is a more expensive way to prepare cats for spay/neuter surgery, and it's not without its risks, but it is hands-down the safest for the cats. Once the surgery is over, the cat wakes up and can start eating within a few minutes. We prefer this type of clinic for any cats that might have a heart condition, for cats that are ill or injured, and for females that might be lactating. More than once, I've left the clinic with a lactating female and, within the hour, returned her to her outdoor home so that she can feed and protect her babies until we can find them.

Post-surgery Care

The question of how to handle the recovery period for cats that have just been spayed or neutered is a fairly controversial topic. The old rule of thumb was that you should hold males for three days after surgery, and females for five. Back when surgery techniques were different and before the days of surgical glue, this might have made sense; now it doesn't. It now seems downright cruel and inhumane.

Keeping ferals confined in traps for days is also terrible for the cats' health. Most of them won't eat or drink while in a trap, and risk dehydra-tion within the first 24 hours after surgery unless they were given subcuta-neous fluids at the clinic. Feral cats also tend to hold their urine for long stretches while in captivity, risking bladder and urinary tract infections. *If you love them, set them free!*

These days, we typically release males the same night of surgery, and females the following morning. Certainly there are exceptions to this practice:

- 🐾 If your spay/neuter clinic administers a vaccine "cocktail" (described previously), sometimes the males are too loopy to release the same night. We hold them until the next morning.

- 🐾 If a female hasn't urinated yet, keep her until she does. In one incident, a suture slipped and closed off a cat's bladder. Before we could figure out what had happened, she died. A female that hasn't urinated within 24 hours of surgery should be taken back to the clinic to make sure that nothing is wrong.

Cats who are injured or ill and therefore must be held in captivity for a few days should be run into floor cages rather than holding them in traps. Ironically, feral cat caregivers who sometimes hold cats in small traps for such a long time that it's actually inhumane, will often choose floor cages that are too *large* for cats to feel secure long term. The best size floor cage for convalescing cats is two feet wide by two feet tall by three feet long.

Arrangement of a floor cage for housing a feral cat.

Before running any feral cat into a floor cage, be sure to cover the cage with a sheet that, once the cat is inside, will *completely* cover all sides of the cage. Set up the inside of the cage in advance; you won't want to be putting your hands into the cage until the cat has had several hours to settle down. Place bowls with dry food and water and a plate of canned food along one side of the interior. Put about two inches of natural clumping litter (made from wheat or corn) into a medium-sized litter box and sprinkle some dirt over the top so that the cat clearly knows where to "go." (Don't try to use potting soil instead of real dirt. Potting soil does not smell like dirt and therefore the cat gets no cues from it.)

Also, for your own convenience as well as for the health of the cat, *never* use clumping clay litter. Thinking that they just might be able to find a way to get out of the cage, feral cats tend to make an absolute mess of the interior during their first 48 hours in captivity. They tip over their water and food bowls and throw litter around the cage. Clumping clay litter will be stuck to everything once it gets mixed with water, and worse yet the cat might ingest some of it that has adhered to the cat's paws or bits of food. The clay then congeals in the cat's stomach and causes intestinal problems later on.

As for getting a cat into a floor cage, the method will depend on what type of container the cat is in. If you did your homework when you caught the cat and knew that it was sick and would need medication for a few days, then hopefully you had the foresight to take a carrier to the spay/neuter clinic along with the cat. Most veterinarians are amenable to placing a feral cat into a small carrier (rather than the trap in which it arrived) for recovery after surgery. If that's the case, then you can simply put the carrier into the floor cage and open the door. I put a folded towel or cozy cat bed on top of the carrier so that the cat can rest there if it wants to. Otherwise, the interior of the carrier gives the cat a safe place to hide until night when your home is quiet and the cat feels safe enough to eat and use the litter box.

One cautionary note: when working with a cat that is particularly violent, I use a towel to protect my hand while unlatching any trap or carrier door. With a carrier inside a floor cage, after unlatching the carrier door, I close the cage door and then use a broom handle to swing the carrier door open and release the cat into the cage. It's always better to be safe than bleeding!

A trap-to-cage transfer will be necessary for cats that come home from the spay/neuter clinic in traps. This can be hair-raising – every single movement must be double checked to avoid the cat's getting loose. In other words, if you're not in hyper-alert mode while making this type of transfer, then something is wrong. No matter how often I do it, my heart still pounds and my hands shake until it's over.

The general principle of this type of transfer is that a cat will always move from an *uncovered* area to a *covered* area. Thus, with your floor cage set up and covered with a sheet, you're going to uncover the trap so that the cat will move into the covered floor cage.

To accomplish this, rest the edge of the end of the trap on the edge of the cage opening nearest the door hinge. Then, using two pieces of stiff cardboard, block the open spaces between the top and side of the trap and the cage. An important step is to place one foot sideways against the lower piece of cardboard to hold it tight to the frame of the floor cage. I omitted this step once and the cat was able to see a sliver of light; it bolted through the cardboard, got onto a windowsill in my bedroom, and in its panic to escape proceeded to destroy the blinds on the window! I had to re-trap her in order to get her safely into the floor cage.

Setting the stage for a trap-to-cage transfer.

With cardboard and trap in place, open the end of the trap. This is one of those situations in which you'll be extremely happy if the trap has a guillotine door at one end. Simply lift the door. Otherwise, you'll have to reach in and pull up the angled trap door and hold it up while the cat moves into the cage, which can be quite tricky to do while keeping the cardboard securely in place.

At this point, remove the towel covering the trap. Resist the temptation to make the cat move into the floor cage quickly, such as by poking it.

A frantic cat is your worst enemy. Within a few minutes (which can sometimes feel like 100 years), the cat will typically move cautiously into the floor cage. Give it an extra moment or two to move to the back of the floor cage. Then with very fluid, steady movements, replace the guillotine door (or close the spring door). Move the trap back just far enough to lower the

A cat won't need much encouragement to move from the uncovered trap into the cozy floor cage.

upper piece of cardboard to completely cover the opening of the floor cage. Then quietly move the trap out of the way, shut the door of the floor cage, slide the pieces of cardboard out, and latch the cage door. Take a big sigh of relief.

While caring for any feral cat in a cage enclosure, it's important to assume a non-threatening posture while you're working. Kneel on the floor before opening the cage – *never* open the cage door or try to change food and water bowls from a standing position. Avoid staring at the cat, which is a sign of aggression. Keep your head tilted slightly downward and blink frequently. Open the door only as far as you need to for actions such as removing or replacing food and water bowls. Stay in tune at all times by watching the cat in your peripheral vision. If you sense that the cat might bolt, then smoothly but quickly close the door and try again later. (In one case, a vet tech that I know swung the door open to replenish food and wasn't watching the cat's signals; the cat took the opportunity to launch itself over her head and out of the cage. She ended up in the hospital emergency room with multiple lacerations to her scalp.)

If the cat has "redecorated" by moving the bowls around or if you must scoop the litter box, move these items within reach by using some-thing like a broom handle. Again, open the cage door only as far as neces-sary to remove each item. If the cat is hiding in the carrier, things will be easier. Simply use a broom handle to swing shut the door of the carrier; reach in and latch it closed; remove the carrier. At this point you will be free to clean the cage and refresh the food and water.

When it comes time to remove a cat from an enclosure that doesn't already contain a carrier, as long as the cat has been spending most of its time at the back of the cage and hasn't tried to lunge at you, take out the litter box and put a small carrier with the door open into the floor cage. (Move *very* gently and fluidly while doing this so as not to scare the cat any more that it already is.) After you've closed and latched the cage door, pull off the sheet that covers the floor cage. In most cases, the cat will immedi-ately scoot into the carrier. Sometimes it helps to leave the area for a few minutes; when you return, the cat will often magically be inside the carrier. If not, then use something long and slender that will fit between the bars of the cage to gently guide it towards the carrier door. Don't use anything as hard as a broom handle, though, because the cat might try to bite it and break a tooth.

Cats that are violent, or that must go to a spay/neuter clinic or veteri-nary appointment, should be run into a trap from the cage. Simply reverse the trap-to-cage transfer process previously described. If you have any doubt as to whether the cat should go into a carrier or into a trap, then a trap should be your choice as it's by far the safest means to use for trans-porting a feral cat.

We have held many feral cats using the techniques described here. A recent situation involved a female with an eye injury; the veterinarian sewed a flap over the cat's eye to protect it while it healed. At first, it was suggested that we hold the cat for two weeks. Later, because the cat was doing relatively well in its cage, the veterinarian requested that we hold it for one more week to be sure that the eye had healed as much as possible. We were all thrilled when she removed the stitches and found that the eye had healed perfectly.

Feral mothers can be kept with their kittens in floor cages, also – but we tend to use a larger cage so that the mother can stretch out to nurse her kittens. If the kittens are less than two weeks old, we put the kittens into the cage first and then put the mother in, being extremely careful to keep the cat calm during the transfer process so that she doesn't hurt her babies. With older kittens, we run the mother into the cage, and then put the kittens in one by one. For some reason, this seems to help the mother "recognize" her kittens; in a couple of cases, mothers lashed out upon encountering their kittens in a cage as though they were random, strange beings.

A feral Mom relaxes with her kittens in a floor cage.

Incidentally, it's a good idea to get the mother cat spayed when the kittens are between four to six weeks of age in order to minimize the possibility that she will go into heat again. This is relatively safe for both kittens and Mama as long as isoflurane is the only anesthesia used during the surgery. Let the veterinarian know that the mother will continue to nurse her kittens after the surgery so that appropriate vaccines can be administered.

Kitten Evaluation and Care

Typically, feral cat trapping requests come in when a mother cat and kittens have shown up in a residential backyard or the parking lot of a cat-lover's place of employment. While the spay/neuter process for adult cats is relatively cut-and-dried, any situation that involves kittens means extra effort and thoughtful decision making.

The first step is to figure out who will foster any kittens produced by the trapping efforts. Will you have time to do this yourself? Or will you need to rely on a fellow cat rescuer to help? While I realize that most cat rescuers have busy lives, it's important to do some soul-searching about the extent to which you should be trapping if you are unable to foster kittens yourself. Given the limited resources of all cat rescue groups, it's important for each person to see their trapping efforts through from start to finish.

And which kittens should get fostered? Some cat rescuers think that only "bottle babies" (kittens under four weeks old) are worth pulling from the wild. Others limit their efforts to kittens up to eight weeks old. Some people don't bother trapping kittens at all, and instead wait until they're old enough to spay or neuter and return to the colony.

I happen to be of the opinion that all kittens four *months* old and younger should be removed from feral colonies if possible. This is a fairly controversial topic on which not everyone agrees with me – even people within my own rescue community. But I'm convinced that *it is the most humane and conscientious way to deal with kittens* from any feral cat environment.

The best way to explain my perspective is to offer a story about a local retirement community. A resident started feeding a handful of feral cats, and in the spring two females showed up with kittens in tow. The community board of directors demanded that the feeders withhold nourishment and that the cats be removed from the property, or else the feeders would face eviction. With heavy hearts, the feeders started trapping and caught a kitten, which they surrendered to the local humane society.

Luckily, I was there that morning. It was too late to prevent the kitten from being admitted to the shelter, but when I learned more about the story, I requested a "hold" on the kitten (which meant that the shelter staff could not euthanize her for behavioral issues and would have to give her back to me after a four-day waiting period) and went to work helping the feeders. All of the kittens were brought to my foster home, and all of the adults got spayed and neutered. We quietly returned the adults to the colony, and the feeders learned to be more discreet by placing food under the eaves of the building rather than near a walkway.

Once the board members at the retirement community saw that the number of cats was reduced by more than 50% and that the cats were completely quiet (no yowling or other mating noises), they agreed to let them stay.

While I'm well aware of the strain that kittens can place on any cat rescue organization, it is our duty to get as many cats as possible off the streets. The fewer free-roaming cats, the more tolerant the community will be about letting them live out their natural lives in peace. And why should feeders spend years providing nourishment to cats that could have been removed from colonies when they were young? The long-term financial burden on rescue groups for food and veterinary care doesn't make sense when kittens can be placed into permanent homes.

The same goes for stray adults – if a cat meows in the trap and you are brave enough to try to pet it, you might find out that it's quite a nice cat. In that case, consider asking the spay/neuter clinic to leave the ears intact, and see if you can find some generous, patient soul to foster the cat. *We need to get as many cats as possible off the streets.*

Thus, when I'm trapping and have caught a kitten, my first thought is NOT spay/neuter. Basically, if you want a kitten to become your friend at some point, don't start off your relationship by containing it in a trap, carting it off to a chaotic veterinary clinic, and making it sit there for hours with no food or water.

Instead, my first actions entail getting kittens settled and starting the process of acclimating them to humans, the latter of which there are two methods. One is to gradually entice kittens to come to you, for which I have absolutely no patience (it does, however, generally produce more universal and long-lasting results). The other is to get your hands on the kittens early and often. This is my preferred method because I just can't resist the chance to reassure and comfort a hissing, spitting kitten. They're scared and it's my job to make them unafraid and calm as quickly as possible.

A small room is your best friend when you have a kitten in a trap – especially when you are first attempting some of the handling techniques described here. In a small room, if the kitten escapes, your chances are better of catching it quickly and without harm to either one of you. In other words, don't practice these methods in the middle of your kitchen floor like I do!

When preparing to handle feral kittens, it's important to dress for the occasion. I put on a light sweatshirt, and a second heavier sweatshirt over that. This enables you to quickly put a fearful, squirming kitten between the layers of your clothing and hold it next to your diaphragm (which is basically located in the triangular area at the bottom center of your rib cage). The combination of warmth, darkness, and the sound of your heartbeat will almost immediately make a fearful kitten docile, or at least calm it down.

Please note that it is *not* a good idea to wear leather gloves when handling ferals, whether adults or kittens. I've tried it a couple of times and have been bitten every time. Sharp cat teeth easily penetrate leather! I'm not sure what it is about gloves that provokes a cat to bite, but my guess is that two factors come into play – the smell of the gloves (a combination of earthy and meaty), and they know that it's not your "real" hand (cats truly don't want to bite you if they don't have to).

Pushing a towel through a partially opened guillotine door.
(The towel that was covering the trap was removed for the purposes
of this photo. Leave the towel in place when trying this technique.)

To get a kitten out of a trap, sit cross-legged and put whichever end of the trap you'll be opening in your lap, with the far end resting on the floor. Have a medium-sized towel close by. Pull back the end of the towel that's covering the trap, and get a good look at the kitten. If it's small, I often just reach in with my bare hands and grab it by putting one hand over its shoulders with my thumb and middle finger behind the front legs, exerting a moderate amount of pressure against the rib cage. This has a similar effect to scruffing (you'll notice the kitten's rear legs curling up towards its stomach), but works much better and gives you more control. Quickly stick the kitten between your sweatshirts, as described previously.

If the kitten is too frantic or too old to grab with your bare hands, then for the safety of all concerned, use that towel that you've placed nearby. Open the end of the cage a little over an inch, and start pushing the towel into the trap. This takes a few moments, because you don't want to open the trap door far enough for the kitten to sense an avenue for escape. Once the entire towel is inside the trap, then move one hand in and let the guillotine door rest against your arm. With fingers spread apart, hold the towel so that it creates a vertical wall inside the trap, and move it slowly towards the kitten. With the towel against the kitten and keeping the towel between you and the kitten at all times, tuck the towel over the kitten's head.

When the kitten can't see daylight any longer, it should stop squirming and won't be able to see your movements. This is the time to act more quickly and firmly, tucking the towel around the sides and back end of the kitten's body. Grab the edges of the towel and you should now be able to remove the kitten from the trap like the mythical stork carrying a baby.

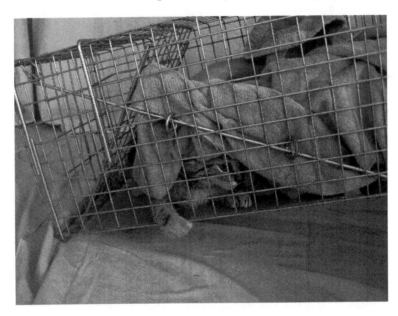

Tucking a towel around the head of a feral kitten. (Keep the trap covered with a towel when trying this technique.)

With the kitten in the towel, I sit in the bathroom and have nail clippers, magnifying glasses ("readers"), a flea comb, and Advantage® at hand. First I expose only the kitten's face, keeping the towel tucked snugly around its neck and body. This gives me a good chance to assess whether the kitten has any medical issues, such as ringworm, ear mites, or an upper respiratory infection.

Next, I re-cover the head with the towel, and one-by-one pull out the kitten's little paws and trim its nails. After that, with the entire rest of the body covered by the towel, I expose the back end and find out whether it's male or female. If the kitten isn't squirming too badly at this point, I'll move the towel up a bit and flea comb the hind quarters in order to gauge the number of fleas on the kitten. Then I cover the body again, expose the head, and apply Advantage at a dosage of one drop per estimated pound of weight. In my experience, this has been safe and effective for kittens between four and eight weeks of age. (Do not use any other type of flea medication on kittens this young, especially the over-the-counter types sold at pet stores. It could kill them.)

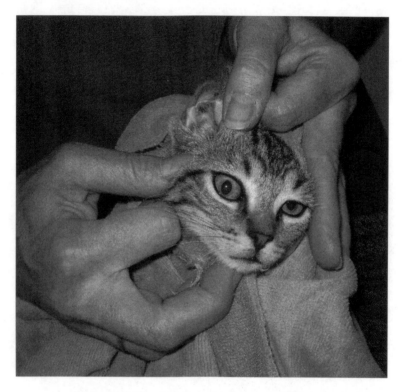

Examining a feral kitten's ears. Finger placement allows light pressure to be applied to the head, lower neck and front of the shoulder blades, helping to keep the kitten still and the towel snugly in place.

After accomplishing all of this initial work, I wrap the kitten completely in the towel again and place it in a medium-sized dog crate or floor cage with dry food, canned food, water, and a litter box. Placing the dog crate on a table or countertop so that the kitten is at human-body level is extremely helpful in the socialization process, making the Giant Ones seem much less intimidating.

Dog crate set-up for a newly trapped feral kitten.

Over the next few days, reach in as often as possible to pet the kitten. The frequency of interaction is far more important than the length of time spent on each interaction. Usually you will know within a week or two whether you will eventually be able to socialize the kitten and place it up for adoption.

Some people ask me what the age cut-off point is for socializing versus returning kittens to their colonies. Sorry to say, there's no answer. I've seen six-week-old kittens barely adjust to the presence of humans even after several months of socialization efforts, and I've had five-month-old kittens start purring for me within hours of being trapped. What I *can* tell you is that you should never make a decision during the first 48 hours of captivity. Give the kitten a chance.

This should go without saying, but once they are socialized, be sure to get kittens spayed and neutered before putting them up for adoption. Much research has been done at this point on the benefits and minimal risk of early spay/neuter surgeries; there should be no reason whatsoever for adopting out kittens when they are still intact. This has the added benefit of insuring that feral cat rescuers maintain a reputation for being part of the solution rather than potential contributors to the problem.

Overall, calm and patience will be rewarded when working with feral cats and kittens. Avoid the tendency to think like a human, and instead try to think like a feline. Every step of the way, make sure to keep cats calm and feeling protected. Do not let them see any chance to escape until you're ready to release them back into their outdoor homes (cats) or move them into an enclosure (kittens).

One of my fellow rescuers says that releasing adult feral cats that have been spayed or neutered is her favorite part of the rescue process – seeing them burst out of the trap or carrier to freedom. *If you love them, set them free.*

CHAPTER 3

TIPS FOR VETERINARY CARE PROVIDERS

Working with feral cats – and sometimes with "social" ones as well – can be exceptionally difficult. Cats are territory oriented, so even the friendliest can turn scared and sometimes hostile on alien turf such as a veterinary clinic.

Time and again, I see both technicians and veterinarians "scruff" kittens and even adult cats. They seem to feel that this will calm or immobilize the cat. In my experience, this is rarely necessary and can give the false impression of control. There are safer ways to proceed, both for the caregivers and the cats.

Keeping Cats Calm

Before you even get to the stage of handling a frightened or feral cat, the first step to take is to make sure that the waiting period is as quiet and dark as possible. Cover carriers and traps *completely* with a towel or sheet – no daylight should show from any side. Place the carriers or traps out of the way of human noise and foot traffic.

When you are ready to handle a cat that is not feral but is scared, there is a technique that seems quite logical to me but that I have found is counter-intuitive for others. ALWAYS remove a reluctant cat from a carrier hind-end first. It's also good to put such cats back into their carriers the same way. Whichever way you're going, cradle the cat's body between your forearms and put your index and middle fingers around the pair of legs that are entering the carrier. (In other words, put your fingers around the cat's front legs if you're removing the cat from the carrier, and around the hind legs if you're putting a cat into a carrier.)

The Towel Trick

The "towel trick" described for getting kittens out of traps in the previous section is undoubtedly the most useful tool in my cat-handling arsenal. I use it often, not only on kittens but also sometimes with semi-feral adult cats. In our local rescue clinic, I even use it with social cats who turn nasty when facing medical treatment.

Recently, during a spay/neuter clinic event, I used the towel trick on four separate cats. One was someone's pet, and the vet tech took it out of the recovery cage by scruffing it. The cat freaked out at the sight of the carrier and got away from the tech, bouncing off the walls of the clinic. I waited for it to pause on a windowsill, got a towel over it, kept my left hand over the rib cage with a slight downward pressure, tucked the towel around the head with my right hand, and then tucked in all of the sides. I put the cat in the carrier towel and all. Once the door was closed, I slowly pulled the towel out while keeping the door open only a crack.

The second cat was someone's pet and she was downright violent under the stress of being at the clinic. I used the towel trick to get her out of the carrier, and after surgery we bypassed the recovery cage and let her wake up right in her carrier. The third and fourth cats were feral but had arrived at the clinic in carriers rather than traps, making transfer to the anesthesia chamber tricky. The buggers refused to budge out of the carriers and were relatively small cats, so I just used the towel trick. Worked like a charm.

An interesting point to note is one that was taught to me by a veterinarian who is an internal medicine specialist. He told me that there are basically two types of cats – those that lash out when they're scared, and those that shrink back. In the situations just described, you can see that the first two cats were social cats of the type that lashes out; the second two were feral cats, but of the kind that shrinks back. These are perfect candidates for the towel trick – but I *never use it on violent, truly feral cats.*

The towel trick helps keep scared cats calm even when giving fluids or trimming nails. To give subcutaneous (commonly abbreviated as "sub-Q") fluids, keep the towel covering the cat and simply pull one side up to expose the cat's shoulder and administer the fluids. Cats that are resistant to nail trimming can usually be handled by using a towel and starting with the *back* feet first.

One friend's cat – an obese female ironically named Twiggy – was completely violent; no one had ever trimmed her nails without her being under sedation. I used the towel trick and even though she squirmed and screamed as though I was torturing her, I was able to get the back feet done rather quickly. The front feet were another matter.

In desperation, with the towel still completely covering Twiggy, I put her down on the floor. Next, I rolled a washcloth so that it was in the shape of a fat cigar, and placed this under her chin so that she couldn't get her mouth open far enough to bite me. Loosely holding the washcloth in place with my wrist, I picked up each of her front feet one by one and was able to trim the nails. She wailed through the whole process, but luckily the Super-bowl was on television that day and my friend had the sound turned up quite high. No one reported me to the authorities for animal abuse, and everyone survived the experience.

Using an Anesthesia Chamber

The process of getting a feral cat into an anesthesia chamber is actually quite a bit easier than getting one into a floor cage, but some of the same principles and techniques apply. At our local rescue clinic, I *always* do this in the bathroom for the same reasons described in the section on working with feral kittens.

First, place the carrier on its side with the bottom (which is now the side) against something firm such as a wall. This prevents the cat from pushing the chamber as it enters and creating a means for escape. Cover all sides except the opening with a towel. Rest the lid at an angle against the opening of the chamber, making sure that the vent pipes are on the side of the lid farthest away from the chamber.

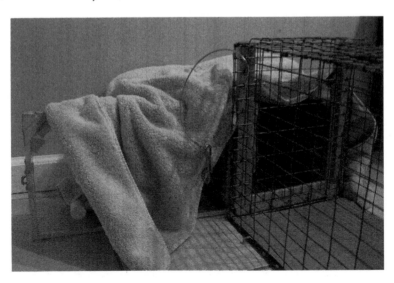

A trap is lined up against an anesthesia chamber,
which is covered with a towel. The lid of the chamber
can be seen on the left side of the photo.

Position the opening of the trap against the open half of the chamber and place one foot behind the end of the trap to immobilize it. With fluid movements but in relatively quick succession, 1) open the trap door, 2) remove the towel that covers the trap, and 3) grab the lid handle of the chamber. Let the cat move at its own pace into the chamber; do not try to rush it. As soon as most of its body is in the chamber, tilt the trap slightly to the side so that you can slide the lid into place.

Similar to many of the techniques described in this book, it is extremely important to try this with a non-violent but skittish cat before trying it with a true feral. Use caution at all times.

In rare cases, we will have a cat arrive at the spay/neuter clinic in a carrier. It is much more difficult to move feral cats from carriers into an anesthesia chamber, mostly because cats feel protected in the carrier and there is no way to "expose" them in the same way as removing a towel that covers a trap. In addition, the opening of the carrier is often much larger than the entrance to the anesthesia chamber, giving the cat an avenue for escape. In these cases, similar to the technique for running feral cats into holding cages described previously, I use a stiff piece of cardboard to cover any gaps. If the cat won't budge from the back of the carrier, coax it via gentle prodding with a tongue depressor or a chopstick.

While some veterinarians use the "noose" (around the chest) method, among others, to handle feral cats, the techniques described here produce more consistent results and are much safer for cats and handlers alike. By reducing trauma for the cats during their time at the clinic, we correspondingly speed up their recovery and release back into the wild.

Here's to the well being and safe handling of all feral and otherwise skittish cats!

CHAPTER 4

FOSTERING KITTENS

There is plenty of guidance concerning bottle babies (orphan kittens that are so young they need to be fed by bottle) available on the Internet and in books, so the care of very young kittens will not be covered in this section. But there can be some tricky health issues to deal with in older kittens, and the expense of medical care can be overwhelming. This section offers guidance on managing both.

Routine Medical Care

The biggest challenge in rescuing kittens over the age of five weeks is that, because they're old enough to have been mobile and eating from communal food sources with other cats, they have had the chance to be exposed to a variety of ailments. Unless you are fortunate enough to be independently wealthy, the costs of traditional veterinary care will add up quickly and you will be forced to halt your rescue efforts.

There are, however, many things that you can do to hold down expenses. The most obvious is to affiliate yourself with a local cat rescue group – or start your own – and get donations to cover some of the expense.

Be sure to take advantage of low-cost spay/neuter clinics. Not only are most of them subsidized and thus less expensive than traditional veterinary clinics, but because the staff veterinarians do these surgeries *all the time* they are much faster at it. Thus each cat or kitten will be under anesthesia for a shorter amount of time, lessening the risk of complications.

Another way to lower expenses is to learn how to do routine, life-saving procedures on your own. The three most important are pilling, giving FRVCP (feline rhinotracheitis-calici-panleukopenia) vaccines, and administering subcutaneous (sub-Q) fluids.

Most veterinarians are willing to show cat rescuers how to give FVRCP vaccines, which are available without a prescription. These offer kittens a certain amount of immunity against the major viruses that have either been passed along to them by their mothers, or that the kittens might encounter in other cats. Purchase the vaccines and needles directly from a veterinary wholesaler, or perhaps your veterinarian will agree to sell them to you at cost. My rescue veterinarian recommends the "three-in-one" FVRCP vaccine described in the previous paragraph. Some veterinarians use "four-in-one" vaccines that include protection against chlamydia, but we have found that kittens can have a strong negative reaction to this type of vaccine.

The vaccines must be kept in the refrigerator at all times, and come in two parts – the vaccine powder, and the sterile diluent. We use a 3-cc syringe with a 23-gauge needle to draw the diluent out of one bottle and insert it into the bottle of powder. This process of poking the needles into the hard rubber stoppers on the tops of the bottles greatly dulls the needles. Your kittens will hardly notice the procedure if, once the reconstituted vaccine liquid is in the syringe, you exchange the 23-gauge needle for a fresh 25-gauge one. (Some veterinarians scoff at changing the needles. Let them! Try it yourself and see the difference. You really have to push hard to get a dull 23-gauge needle to pierce a kitten's skin.)

Another item that can be purchased without a prescription is Drontal®, a broad-spectrum de-wormer. Typically it must be purchased by the bottle (50 tablets), but the cost savings is worth it. Again, if you partner with other rescuers, purchasing in such a large quantity shouldn't be a problem. De-worm kittens when they have reached at least 1.5 pounds in weight. (If you suspect that a kitten has roundworms and it doesn't yet weigh 1.5 pounds, use Strongid or Nemex instead.)

Purchasing the de-worming pills is one thing; getting the pills down the kittens' throats is another matter. Drontal is extremely bitter. If the kitten bites down on the pill, or if some of the medicine gets onto its tongue, the kitten will likely foam at the mouth for several minutes. Syringe-feeding some water to the kitten at this point will only make things worse. (Get some chicken baby food into the kitten's mouth instead.)

In terms of getting bitter medicine into kittens, "pill pockets" (found at most pet stores) are your best friends – but in most cases, you can't just put the pill into the pocket and expect the kitten to eat it. Pill pockets are the consistency of dough. Pull off a very small amount and wrap it around the piece of Drontal, forming a thin coating that smoothes out any rough edges and seals in any powder that formed from breaking the pill into the appropriate size. (For example, the dosage for a two-pound kitten is one-half pill; breaking the pill in half creates a thin layer of dust on the raw edge.)

Your index finger must be completely dry in order to give medicine that's coated with pill pocket dough; otherwise the pill pocket matter will stick to your finger. It will also help if your fingernail is fairly short, because it might get lodged in the dough and the pill then won't make it down the kitten's throat.

Take the kitten into the bathroom, sitting on the toilet with the lid closed. To administer the pill, first make sure to hold the kitten in such a way that the kitten won't be able to move backwards, which is the typical response once you start the procedure. I find it easiest to block the path by putting the crook of my elbow behind the kitten's rear. Next, put the palm of that hand on the top of the kitten's head with your index finger and thumb firmly holding the kittens cheekbones (just below the outer corners of the eyes). Tipping the head upwards, use the fingernail of the middle finger on the other hand to catch the lower front teeth and pull down the lower jaw. Toss the pill directly into the center back of the tongue, and quickly give it a little push with your index finger. Have a syringe filled with water ready, and quickly squirt some into the side of the kitten's mouth. This not only helps the kitten to swallow the pill quickly, but it assures that the pill will travel to the stomach rather than getting stuck in the esophagus. (Chasing pills with water is important to do with adult cats, too.)

Practice makes perfect on pilling, but once you've gotten the hang of it, it's easy. There have been times when I've had a litter or two of kittens that were all sick at once, and everyone needed to be pilled twice daily. I now can literally pill a kitten a minute!

One last note on administering de-wormers concerns the follow-up doses. If your funds are tight and you saw no evidence of roundworms (squirmy things that look like angel-hair pasta; sometimes the kittens throw them up, but usually they come out with the stool) after the first pilling, then it's probably not necessary to worm the kitten again. If you do see roundworms, though, then you absolutely *must* pill the kitten again in *exactly* three weeks.

If you ask a veterinarian about subsequent doses, or read the instructions on the bottle of Drontal, you'll get all kinds of guidance – repeat after 2 weeks – no, 4 weeks! But what I learned from an internal medicine specialist is the three-week trick. My understanding of what he told me is that when roundworms are present, any de-wormer kills only the adults; not the eggs. In three weeks, those eggs will be "teenagers" that are old enough to be killed with the de-wormer, but not so old that they have begun depositing eggs again. I've found this to be true – when I first started using Drontal, I was told that it should be administered every two weeks. But the roundworms came back. And if I forgot the three-week mark and de-wormed a kitten again after four weeks, the worms came back. So the three-week time regimen is the key.

Unfortunately, de-worming can create some intestinal trauma for kittens, especially those that had roundworms. Time and again, I've de-wormed kittens and the next thing you know, the kittens are vomiting and have diarrhea. This is one of those occasions in which you'll be relieved to be able to give sub-Q fluids. Many veterinarians and veterinary technicians will be happy to show you how to tell if a kitten is dehydrated, and how to administer fluids.

There are several different techniques for giving fluids to kittens, but my preference is to use a 23-gauge butterfly needle (technically called a "winged infusion set") attached to a 35-cc or 50-cc syringe. Many veterinarians give cold fluids to cats and kittens, but things will go easier if you warm them first. With kittens, in particular, the shock of feeling even warm fluids entering under the skin can make them jump. The needle then pops out, fluids spray all over the place, and you have to start again. Imagine the reaction if the fluids were cold! Trust me: warm the fluids.

Some people have told me that they don't like the idea of sticking a needle in a kitten to give either vaccines or fluids. But I can assure you that you'll be thankful for the skill when you go to check on a litter of kittens just before you head for bed and find splatters of diarrhea and pools of vomit all over the place. At the very least, being able to administer sub-Q fluids buys you time to keep the kittens alive and get them to the veterinarian the next morning.

Often, when a kitten has gastro-intestinal trauma such as after being de-wormed, the veterinarian will prescribe metronidazole. This is an inexpensive antibiotic that resolves general bacterial imbalances in the gut; it also has an anti-inflammatory effect. Keeping a bit of metronidazole on hand is the key to getting kittens through tough times, especially when such episodes occur on weekends or late at night, until you can get to the clinic. Using pill pockets to administer the medicine will help in this case, also, because metronidazole crumbles easily and is bitter. (For additional information on metronidazole, see the section on infectious diseases in Chapter 4.)

With these skills of pilling, giving vaccines, and administering sub-Q fluids, you can keep expenses at a minimum. For example, a visit to a veterinarian for vaccines and de-worming for a litter of four kittens can cost well over $200. By purchasing the necessary medicines and equipment and doing it yourself, it will cost about $40. On top of that, you should rarely incur the expense of an overnight hospital stay (usually over $100) if you perfect the skill of giving fluids (about $1.50 per dose, including the cost of the drip line and needles).

Coping with Infectious Diseases

Sadly, giving a kitten an FRVCP vaccine does not mean that it will not get sick. In most cases, older foster kittens have been removed from their mother's care – and thus from getting her antibodies through her milk. It is very common for kittens to come down with *something* during their first four weeks in captivity.

The most common illness we see is usually referred to as an "upper respiratory infection" and is caused by the feline herpes virus. This is what the "rhinotracheitis" component of the vaccine is supposed to protect against, and among the other cat rescuers that I talk with, it's one of the least understood ailments of kittens and cats. It commonly erupts just after a kitten has attended an adoption fair or just after it has been spayed or neutered, so rescuers often blame the eruption on other rescuers' kittens or on the spay/neuter clinic. However, as one veterinarian said to me, "It's futile to blame an upper respiratory infection on anyone. Eighty to ninety percent of cats carry this virus, so in most cases it has been passed to the kittens by their mothers." As soon as the kittens are stressed, here it comes!

Symptoms of an upper respiratory infection include sneezing and a fever. (Calici, protection against which is also part of the FVRCP vaccine, is yet another type of upper respiratory infection. The easiest way to tell a herpes infection from calici is by looking in the mouth – calici causes red sores.) A few sneezes from one kitten will often trigger an outbreak among every cat in the room. At that point, many rescuers panic and fear that every cat in the house will get sick.

You can try to isolate the sick kitten, but in my experience the damage has already been done by the time you notice the kitten is sneezing. The best course of action is to immediately give any cats or kittens in the area L-lysine powder. This is an amino acid that helps the feline immune system fight back against the herpes virus. The dosage per cat or kitten is 500 mg once daily, stirred into canned cat food or chicken baby food, for two to six weeks. Many health food stores carry lysine, whether in loose powder form or premeasured and enclosed in capsules. Do not buy tablets, though; even if you crush them up, they don't seem to work as well.

Keep an eye on everyone as time passes. Dehydration can be a problem in really young kittens, due to sneezing so much liquid out their noses. Appetite can be a problem if a kitten's nose gets stuffed up, because the kitten can't smell its food. Look closely when each kitten sneezes; if the discharge has turned white, it means an infection is likely on its way. Yellow or green discharge means that a "secondary infection" has set in and the kitten will need antibiotics in order to recover. But if the discharge is clear, please do not drive your veterinarian crazy by asking for medicine. Just as with a human cold, it will take a while to pass – in some cases, up to six weeks.

Speaking of a lack of appetite, any time a kitten is not eating you should probably force-feed it until it starts eating on its own again. Most of us use chicken baby food mixed with a bit of water and administer it with a syringe. In some cases, a kitten won't eat or will forget to eat and you will find it, completely limp, lying on the floor of the cage. This is often due to a drop in blood sugar. Rub some corn syrup on its gums or, if you don't have any of that on hand, get some kitten milk replacer (which typically contains a fair amount of sugar) into its mouth. Within an hour or so, the kitten will probably be fine. But this tendency for young kittens to go into hypoglycemic shock is the main reason why we regularly force-feed any kitten that isn't eating on its own.

Another cause for a kitten "going down" (being completely lethargic or limp) is what in my opinion is the most horrible cat disease of all – panleukopenia, which is sometimes referred to as distemper or parvo. Many shelters routinely euthanize all cats that have possibly been exposed to parvo due to the extremely high risk of contagion and the low survival rate of infected cats. My rescue home has now been hit by it twice, two and a half years apart. Kittens *will* die, and you will feel very lonely because no one wants to visit your home and then take this disease home to their own cats, and no veterinarians want this disease in their clinics. In many ways, you're on your own.

As one experienced and supportive veterinarian said, though, "You *will* survive this. It's mostly good nursing care." (And good sterilization procedures.)

Parvo is fairly easily contained once you know what you're dealing with. The trouble comes in figuring out that your kittens have it before too many other kittens and cats are exposed. There is almost no such thing as "typical" symptoms, and the symptoms mimic those of other ailments. The virus is hardy and can be transmitted from kitten to kitten on your clothing or a toy before you even realize its presence.

The first sign that you might be dealing with parvo is a lack of appetite (which is true of many kitten illnesses). Then you might notice lethargy (also true of other illnesses). There might or might not be diarrhea and dehydration. The classic sign of parvo (although it occurs with salmonella as well) is a kitten hanging its head over the edge of the water bowl. Have your veterinarian run a fecal test *immediately*. There's literally not a second to waste!

If the test confirms the presence of parvo, you must go into immediate action and implement full sterilization procedures in your entire home. Wear a smock every time you handle the infected kittens; hang it outdoors when you're not wearing it. Buy a couple of boxes of latex or nitrile gloves and change them every time you touch anything that you think could be contaminated. Begin washing everything possible with a 1:32 solution of bleach and water. Use a different litter scoop for every box in your home, and bleach each one often.

In the meantime, learn from your veterinarian how to care for any kittens or cats that are ill. Some are going to die in your arms; it will be horrible. My veterinarian suggested giving sub-Q fluids once daily, with an injectable antibiotic put into the fluid pad. Kittens that are not vomiting can sometimes handle an oral antibiotic as well.

Most people believe that if a kitten has had an FVRCP vaccine, it won't get parvo. Unfortunately, that's not the case. It might help fight off the virus, but I've seen eight-week-old kittens survive that had only been vaccinated after we knew that parvo was present in their cage, and I've seen seven-*month*-old kittens die who had already received a series of two or even three vaccines. What no veterinarian has been able to explain is that each time my foster home has been hit by parvo, *no more than two kittens per cage have died*. My theory is that the kittens' immune systems weakened the virus somehow, so that by the time it was passed to the third or fourth kitten, it was easily fought off. I should also mention that in neither case were any kittens present that were younger than eight weeks old.

Little Ahab, from the first litter of parvo kittens,
survived the virus and eventually got adopted.

The first time my home was hit by parvo, it was brought in by a litter of kittens that had been living under a house with their mother. Apparently, as soon as we removed them from her care (and her antibodies via nursing), their own immune systems could not fight off the virus. In the end, two of these three original kittens died, and a total of 16 other cats and kittens in my foster home contracted the virus. But only four kittens out of the 16 exposed cats and kittens died, for a total of six deaths.

The second time we had parvo, it was brought in by a solo kitten that was four months old. This time, because of quick reaction on the cleaning side, only ten kittens were affected. Still, six died; most of them in my arms.

In terms of nursing care, some of the things I've learned about surviving parvo are:

- Never give up on a kitten. It might live. Keep up with daily sub-Q fluids and whatever medicines your veterinarian has suggested.
- Depression is common in parvo kittens. If possible, take them outdoors to sit on your lap for petting or force-feeding sessions.
- While kittens might act as though you're torturing them by force-feeding, don't stop. They'll spit out the food at you; just get as much as you can down their throats. In a couple of cases, I've had to force-feed kittens for as long as fourteen days before they would eat on their own. It was worth it; they survived.

Here are some miscellaneous things that I've learned about cleaning when you're trying to get rid of parvo:

- Bleach is effective for only thirty minutes after it is mixed with water. Make small batches.
- Wear gloves when using bleach. The first time parvo hit, I neglected to do this and ended up with alkaline burns on my hands.
- Wash first with soap and water in order to remove all debris; then rinse; then apply the bleach solution.
- In order to kill all parvo, the bleach needs at least ten minutes to work. Whenever possible, allow bleached surfaces to air dry.
- On the other hand, bleach will turn many surfaces (such as linoleum) yellow. In those cases, wipe with the bleach solution, and then dry using a paper towel. It's better than nothing.

You'll know when you've contained the parvo because there will be no new cases for two weeks. (In other words, a two-week waiting period is re-set each time a new case becomes apparent.) Cats and kittens are considered to be "recovered" when they are eating and drinking on their own, even though they can still shed the virus in their feces for a time.

I heard about one case in which a foster parent spent $6,000 of her own money on a litter of kittens that had parvo. She had taken them to a veterinary clinic and paid out of her own pocket for hospitalization, blood transfusions, etc. All but one kitten died. In my first case of parvo, I spent just over $100 to treat 19 kittens and cats. It was a tremendous amount of work and little sleep, but the survival rate was good, most likely due to vigorous cleaning and round-the-clock nursing care.

Treatment for other types of intestinal issues, especially bacterial infections, can be similar to handling parvo. For the most part, feral kittens pick up nasty bacteria when drinking out of water bowls shared with wildlife, such as raccoons. Common bacteria include giardia, coccidia, campylobacter, and salmonella. Unfortunately, each one of these requires unique medication, so the cause of persistent diarrhea *must* be diagnosed via a fecal test. This is probably the most expensive part of feral kitten rescue, because if the simple and inexpensive "ova and parasites plus giardia" fecal panel doesn't show any bacteria detected, you'll have to spend a pretty penny on a PCR (polymerase chain reaction) diarrhea panel. The latter, however, will definitely show which bacteria you're dealing with.

Whenever you notice diarrhea, the first step is to speak with your veterinarian. Sometimes it will be suggested to give the kitten metronidazole to see if that clears it up. One cautionary note is that some veterinarians will give you a compounded, liquid form of this medicine. Although they claim that this is "chicken" or "tuna" flavored, don't fall for it. In liquid form, metronidazole tastes bitter to kittens. If you haven't yet mastered pilling and choose to give the liquid, you risk ruining the relationship you've worked so hard to build with the kitten.

Another point concerning metronidazole is that it has traditionally been prescribed for treating giardia, but we are currently seeing resistance. Instead, we're now using tinidazole, which not only appears to be more effective but works more quickly. Ask your veterinarian about this medicine if you've got a confirmed case of giardia on your hands.

Coping with Other Nasty Stuff

As if viruses, worms, and intestinal bacteria weren't enough, there are other issues that can affect older feral kittens – but at least these can't be passed along from kitten to kitten.

Feral kittens who don't live in a colony that is fed regularly get very hungry, and on top of it they're curious little critters. So Mama Cat goes off hunting, the kittens get hungry, and they get into all kinds of garbage. Within three to five days of trapping them, some will vomit up mysterious items; some produce identifiable evidence of their scrounging. In one case, some kittens that had been rummaging through the dumpster of a Chinese restaurant threw up a couple of those matchstick-shaped pieces of bamboo that they use in Chinese cooking. One kitten from a different location threw up a rock; others have thrown up grass or twigs. A kitten that was living on the grounds of a country club threw up part of a used condom.

(How lovely.) Occasionally a kitten will stop eating due to the turmoil the garbage created in the process of being ejected from the stomach, but more often than not the kitten will suddenly be ravenous. Give plenty of food and be happy the offending matter is out of there!

On a sad note, there is one more illness about which many people are poorly informed, and thus spend buckets of money on tests and procedures, only to have a kitten die. That disease is FIP, and it is not included in the previous section on contagious issues because this is the primary factor about which most people are misinformed: *other kittens cannot contract FIP from a sick kitten.* Period. Death from FIP is caused by genetic factors. Other kittens in the same litter share the same genes and could thus be at risk of dying from the disease, but it can't be passed from kitten to kitten.

Much like trying to identify parvo by symptoms alone, it's very difficult to tell if a kitten is in the process of succumbing to FIP. They typically eat, although not as much as usual. They act like they feel a bit under the weather but not desperately sick. They play, but not as much as a normal kitten. Their fur might appear dull or greasy. Their rate of growth might not be keeping pace with that of their siblings. In other words, most of the symptoms are subtle and vague. The one sign that you're probably dealing with FIP is that a kitten will suddenly spike a very high fever – usually over 105°. We often administer antibiotics at this point, hoping against hope that there is something causing the fever that we can't yet see (such as an abscess). The fever lasts for a day or two and then goes away.

To the best of my knowledge, there is currently no test that can conclusively identify early-stage FIP. The best thing you can do is to watch the kitten carefully and treat any obvious problems (such as unrelated diarrhea), in hopes that the lethargy or slow growth rate is due to those problems. Occasionally I'll take a kitten to the veterinarian and beg her to try to find *some* illness other than FIP. Sadly, she usually can't.

Palliative care is the best way to take care of a kitten that's going down with FIP. Give sub-Q fluids if the kitten is getting dehydrated. Force-feed the kitten if it doesn't seem to be eating enough food. Comfort the kitten with plenty of quiet time in your lap. It's all you can do.

We typically wait until either fluids have built up in the kitten's belly (wet form), or until enough symptoms have appeared to make a dry-form diagnosis (inability to walk; tremors), and then have the kitten euthanized. By the time any of those symptoms have appeared, the kitten has only a few days to live.

Many people ask me, "Why wait to euthanize if you're sure it's FIP?" The answer is that we wait because we don't know for sure until the very last minute, and we pray – hard – that it's something else. FIP is really tough that way.

The extreme likelihood that kittens will develop some kind of medical issue within the first few weeks of capture is the reason why every kitten or cat entering any foster home should go into a cage for at least the first fourteen days. *Do not feel sorry for them and let them run freely.* Parvo can incubate in the body for up to fourteen days, and we've seen plenty of cases in which it erupts on Day 13. In any case, kitties always feel safer when they're in small spaces. Don't skimp on the cage time!

When you encounter medical issues in your foster kittens, having patience is a requirement. People think that you also need a soft heart. But having read through this chapter, "courage" might be the word that comes to mind. There's nothing quite so discouraging as having a tiny kitten die in your arms despite hours and hours – or days and days – of tender loving care. On the other hand, success in bringing a kitten through a major illness is an indescribable feeling.

CHAPTER 5

ADOPTING OUT KITTENS AND CATS

By now you've seen that there is both joy and heartbreak involved in the process of fostering feral kittens. The good side is that it feels great to know that the kittens are safely off the streets. Watching their progress in learning how to trust humans is so rewarding. And nothing matches that special moment the first time a kitten purrs!

Many rescuers, though, get kittens acclimated to the presence of them and their homes, but give up on the next step of socializing them to new people and new places. Trusting others – especially strangers – can be challenging for our little ferals. Rescuers get discouraged and feel sorry for the kittens, knowing that they are having a difficult time. Next thing you know, they decide to keep the kittens, who of course then turn into cats. Suddenly the rescuers realize that they have too many felines and give up on feral rescue.

Although it seems that getting kittens through early life-or-death perils is the most important part of cat rescue, don't diminish your efforts later when it comes to adoption!

Public Venues

Among the available avenues for showcasing adoptable felines, none works well alone. It's important to spread your adoption efforts across both in-person settings, such as adoption fairs, and online venues like CraigsList. For adoption fairs, call some local pet stores and ask if they would allow you to display your foster kitties once each weekend. My experience is that one three-hour adoption fair per week is about all the kitties can handle.

44

Adoption fairs are very stressful for feral rescue kittens, but are a necessary part of both the adoption process and the kittens' social development. During an adoption fair, lean into the cages frequently to pet and reassure your kittens that although the environment might be scary, you're there to protect them and no one will hurt them. You'd be surprised at how much progress they'll make after you've done this for three or four weeks in a row.

Finding homes for shy kittens like these can be challenging.

As for online adoption venues, many rescuers worry about being contacted via anonymous methods (either e-mail or telephone). They think that every crazy person in the universe is going to be trying to reach them. Fortunately, this usually is not the case. And there is a tried-and-true way of interviewing people that will give you a good idea of whether they are suitable adopters for your kittens and cats.

When speaking with potential adopters, it is of course necessary to say a few words about the cat and its personality, but mostly you should ask questions and then listen. Never "press the sale." The best questions to ask are:

1) How many humans are in your home? (More than two humans can be overwhelming for shy cats.)
2) Are there any children in your home? (Children under the age of eight years tend to make jerky movements and loud, sudden noises that will terrify a shy cat.)

3) Have you owned cats before? (People who are good candidates will tell you all about the nineteen-year-old cat that they just had to have put to sleep.)

4) Do you currently have any pets in your home? (This will tell you if adopters have another cat for whom they're trying to find a companion. See the next section on Feline Matchmaking.)

Some rescuers rely on "home visits" to make final decisions about potential adopters. They take the cat to the person's home to make sure that the home is as it was described, and to quickly check for major feline safety issues, such as torn window screens. Home visits are wonderful if you only have a few kittens to place each year and can afford the time and gas money. Occasionally, though, reliance on home visits gives people a false sense of confidence; home visits should never take the place of a thorough interview at the start.

Here's an example of one conversation that I had over the telephone with a potential adopter, whom I turned away. We never got past the first question!

Me: So have you had cats before?
Him: Yeah, one, but it got away.
Me: How'd it get away?
Him: Not sure. I think there was a hole in the wall and it got out.
Me: Did you look for the cat?
Him: Naw.
Me: Well I'm not sure that any of my cats are going to do well in your home, but thanks for calling.

Feline Matchmaking

Over the years, researchers have found that cats are much more social than most people think. In addition, having a buddy can prevent or resolve certain behavior issues in cats. For example, a cat that is clingy and vocalizes frequently might change completely – for the better – with the introduction of a compatible companion.

Although many shelter workers and veterinarians recommend placing cats of the opposite sex together, *it is strongly recommended to pair male cats with males and female cats with females.* The main reason behind this is that adult male and female cats play differently. Males want to wrestle and bite each other's paws and ears. While females will sometimes do this, too, most of them prefer playing chase and tossing toys back and forth. Certainly there are exceptions, and in those rare cases I've agreed to a male/female combo.

At one point, I asked one of the top animal behavior experts why so many people recommend pairing males with females. He said that the only reason is due to *one study* that showed that if there was a problem between two cats, it was more easily remedied if it was a male/female pair. Anecdotally, he reported that existing females can often be hissy during the introduction of a new cat; to avoid having to hand-hold and reassure owners that this is a natural part of the process, shelter workers simply prefer to minimize the occurrence.

In my foster home, male/female interactions are pretty much the only behavior problem that I have. Many of the males, right around the age of 11 months, turn into bullies; particularly with petite females. The bully-boys do things such as staring and assuming an assertive posture, which literally makes the girls cry and run for cover. The next thing you know, the girls are urinating on inappropriate surfaces (such as the kitchen counter) out of fear. Given that it's impossible to tell which male kittens will undergo the bully transformation later, it's best to simply avoid the whole issue by pairing boys with boys and girls with girls.

Something that holds rescuers back from adopting out same-sex pairs is the perception that certain male and female kittens, especially siblings, are "bonded." People assume that because two kittens huddle together for body warmth that they would automatically be a good long-term match. It is better to avoid this assumption, and instead carefully observe kittens and focus on their sexes and personality styles when pairing them as long-term companions.

There are a couple of types of situations in which I will avoid placing any of my foster cats. One is a home in which there are already more than three cats. At the very least, the newcomer will be at the bottom of the pecking order for many years to come. And sometimes, the addition of a new cat will create behavior problems such as spraying in one or more of the existing cats. A fellow rescuer calls this the "exponential addition." It is usually best to hold out for a less crowded home.

The other situation that should be avoided is adopting out a kitten – or even an adult cat – into a home in which there is an existing elderly cat. "Elderly" would be defined in this case as over the age of 15 years. All too often, I've witnessed and heard stories about elderly cats being so stressed by the addition of a new cat that their health declines suddenly and dramatically. It is best to encourage the adopters to wait until their elderly cat crosses the "rainbow bridge" before adopting again.

Preparing Adopters for "Life with Cat"

There are a few important points that I tell every adopter. They involve the most common mistakes that I see people make – even experienced cat owners!

The first matter concerns the morning feeding of a new cat or kitten. It is important that adopters know *not* to feed a cat first thing in the morning when they wake up. Cat owners should get up, have their coffee, take a shower, and then feed the cat. This avoids the life-long, irritating behavior of a cat waking up its owners earlier and earlier each day. It's bad enough that many geriatric cats are a bit senile and might start this behavior late in life. We don't need kittens learning this behavior early!

The second thing that potential adopters should know is that if their kitten is acting frisky, they should not use their hands to play or wrestle with it. Immediately grabbing a toy – especially one of the interactive, "fishing pole"-style toys – is the best way to teach a kitten to play with toys rather than human appendages. Although it's cute when a tiny kitten attacks your finger wiggling under the comforter, it won't be funny when an adult cat attacks your twitching hand in the middle of the night while you're in a deep sleep.

Last but not least, I mention that there are a lot of people who scratch cats at the base of the tail. They believe that the cat enjoys it because it might raise its hind end up, and perhaps will do this while purring. But I warn potential adopters that *scratching a cat at the base of the tail should be avoided completely.* It causes instinctive reactions by the cat, none of which is even remotely related to pleasure; instead, the reactions are related to the mating process. The three major instinctive reactions are: raising the hind end (to get ready for sex), biting (which cats do during sex), and licking (what they do after having sex). In other words, when you scratch a cat at the base of its tail, you are provoking it sexually. Biting is the most dangerous reaction, because cats that react this way to "butt scratches" tend to whip around fast and bite really hard. You just might end up in the hospital!

By the way, if you are ever bitten by a cat, the most important thing is to allow (or force) the wound to bleed as much as possible and then run *cold* water over the area for several minutes. Once you've done that, hopefully you can make it to the computer to read the advice available online about cleaning the wound and seeking medical treatment. Something I've noticed is that whenever I have a new bite or scratch, it's important to avoid putting hand cream on the area for at least 48 hours. For some reason, it tends to allow a mild infection to set in. A dab of triple antibiotic ointment is a much better option.

Given the many risks involved, feral cat rescue is a tremendous amount of work and a true labor of love. Some people become involved simply because they want to take care of one little backyard, stabilizing a small family of cats. Others witness large groupings of cats in public areas and decide to take on larger projects.

Right now, shelters around the country burst at the seams with huge numbers of cats, both social and feral. Many are euthanized. Our communities need help in bringing stray and feral cat populations under control. Each cat that gets spayed, neutered, or removed from the streets brings us one step closer to a world in which all cats are cared for and safe.

Best wishes to the humans who choose to make a difference, on their journeys from trapping through fostering and adoptions.

*Cats can be quite happy in a foster setting, but will
thrive with more personal attention in the right "forever" homes.*

ABOUT THE AUTHOR

Casey Wright has spent a lifetime working with feral and stray cats, first on the dairy farm in the northeast United States where she grew up and now in a residential area on the west coast. She typically traps and/or fosters 100-125 new cats and kittens every year.

She is best known for her ability to catch "untrappable" cats for spay/neuter surgery, and for her work socializing hissy feral kittens that are over the age of eight weeks upon capture.

Questions and comments can be submitted to her blog or addressed to her at caseywrightferals@gmail.com. Please be patient in waiting for a response – the cats in her care come first!

Made in the USA
Middletown, DE
22 November 2018